PROV

MW00977247

FRENCH RIVIERA

Travel Guide Book

A Comprehensive 5-Day Travel Guide to Provence
& the French Riviera & Unforgettable
French Travel

• *Travel Guides to Europe Series* •

Passport to European Travel Guides

❧

Eye on Life Publications

Provence & the French Riviera Travel Guide Book
Copyright © 2017 Passport to European Travel Guides

ISBN 10: 1519149433
ISBN 13: 978-1519149435

~

Other Travel Guide Books by
Passport to European Travel Guides

Top 10 Travel Guide to Italy

Florence, Italy

Rome, Italy

Venice, Italy

Naples & the Amalfi Coast, Italy

Paris, France

Top 10 Travel Guide to France

London, England

Barcelona, Spain

Amsterdam, Netherlands

Santorini, Greece

Greece & the Greek Islands

Berlin, Germany

Munich, Germany

Vienna, Austria

Istanbul, Turkey

Budapest, Hungary

Prague, Czech Republic

Brussels, Belgium

"Is it any better in heaven, my friend Ford, than you found it in Provence?"

—*William Carlos Williams*

Table of Contents

• Map of Provence & the French Riviera •

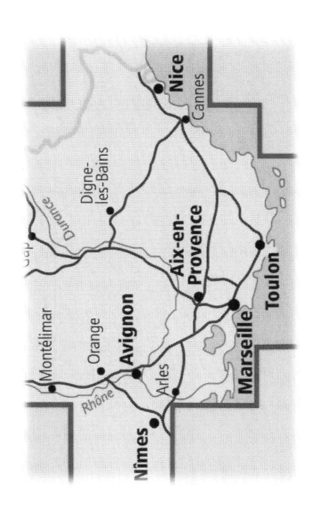

• Introduction •

Provence. **The French Riviera.** Many consider this the most beautiful and visit-worthy locale in all of France. It's been called a playground for the wealthy, a haven for the rich and famous.

Who knows whom you might bump into while you're here?

The gorgeous Mediterranean region from Provence to the French Riviera (a.k.a. la Côte d'Azur) encompasses an impressively wide range of real estate—from the snow-capped mountains of the **Southern French Alps** to the great plains of the **Camargue**, Europe's deepest canyon, the **Gorges du Verdon**, not to mention **Cannes**, **Nice**, **St. Tropez** and **Monaco**.

So unless you have months on your hands to explore the entire area, you'll need to decide exactly where you'd like to **have your adventure**—and we're here to help you choose!

In this 5-day guide to Provence and the French Riviera, you'll get the sharpest recommendations and **tips** to best prepare you with everything you need to know in order to have a most successful and memorable experience!

Be sure to read over the **insider tips** carefully and familiarize yourself with the information so you can pack and prepare accordingly. Every traveler is different, so we've included a variety of information and recommendations to suit all interests and budgets. You can plan according to our **detailed 5-day itinerary,** or you can mix it up and **mix and match your activities** and scheduling. We encourage you to do whatever works for the enjoyment of your trip!

Enjoy!

The Passport to European Travel Guides Team

• City Snapshot •

Language: French

Local Airports:

Western Provence (Avignon, Aix, Arles, Luberon, Ventoux, Camargue) is served by three airports: Avignon Caumont Airport (a small and friendly airport), Nimes Airport, and Marseille-Provence Airport.

Central Provence (Var département, coast from the Rhône to St. Tropez) has two convenient airports: Marseille-Provence Airport and Toulon-Hyères Airport.

The Eastern and Northern-most area of Provence (Digne, Alpes-de-Haute-Provence, Verdon Gorges) are also accessible from Nice-Côte-d'Azur International Airport

Currency: Euro | € (EUR)

Country Code: 33

Emergencies: Dial 112

• Before You Go... •

✓ Have a Passport

If you don't already have one, you'll need **to apply for a passport** in your home country a good two months before you intend to travel, to avoid cutting it too close. You'll need to find a local passport agency, complete an application, take fresh photos of yourself, have at least one form of ID and pay an application fee. If you're in a hurry, you can usually expedite the application for a 2-3 week turnaround at an additional cost.

✓ Need a Visa?

Residents of the US, Mexico and many other countries don't need to apply for a French visa unless they plan to stay in France for longer than **three months (90 days)**. However, citizens of some countries (such as China) need to apply for a visa no matter how long they plan to stay. If you're unsure, just check with your local consulate.

The US State Department provides a wealth of country-specific information for American travelers, including **travel alerts and warnings**, the location of the **US embassy in each country**, and of course, **whether or not you need a visa** to travel there!
http://travel.state.gov/content/passports/english/country.html

✓ Healthcare

Most people neglect this, but it's important to keep in mind when traveling to any foreign country. It's wise to **consult with your doctor** about your travel plans and ensure routine **immunizations** are current. You want to protect against things like influenza, polio, chickenpox, mumps, measles, etc.

And although France's medical system is nationalized and visitor-friendly, it's still advisable to **ensure you'll be covered** when you travel abroad.

✓ Set the Date

Choose the best time for the best experience! The regions of Provence and the French Riviera enjoy **very sunny weather** most of the year. **Spring and autumn** are the best times to travel because temperatures are typically very comfortable this time of year with fewer tourists.

Summertime is full of festivals and the weather is steamy; often quite hot by most standards. Europeans typically vacation in **July and August**, jamming up the Riviera.

September brings the grape harvest, when small wineries are pretty much off-limits to taste-seeking travelers. **Late autumn** delivers beautiful foliage and tranquility.

Although you can experience fairly mild and pleasant weather in any season, Provence is famous for its chilling temperatures in the winter months when the winds blow. **Winter travel** is generally fine in Provence and on the Riviera, but please note: tourist-information offices **keep shorter hours** at this time, and some tourist activities even stop altogether, so when you choose to travel should depend on the types of things you'd like to experience.

And of course, it's always best to **book flights, hotels and train passes** as far in advance as possible for better rates all around.

✓ Pack

Pack well, but don't pack too much! **Leave space** for all the great **shopping** you'll be doing in French Riviera shops! Otherwise, you'll end up having to buy extra luggage and pay those ghastly **baggage fees** on the trip home.

• Make **copies of your travel documents and your passport** and email them to yourself before your trip — that will protect you from a big headache if you lose your documents.

• Since Europe uses **220 volts** of electricity compared to the **110 volts** used in America, travelers from **outside Europe** will need to bring along a **universal electrical plug converter** that can work with both the higher voltage and the differing shape of the electrical plug. This way you'll be able to plug in your cell phones, tablets, curling irons, etc., during the trip **without frying** them since they weren't designed to run on the higher voltage.

• If you don't want to feel **underdressed** in comparison to the French, leave the denim shorts and tennis shoe-type clothing at home—they just scream "tourist!"

Opt for solid colors, slacks and dress shirts, scarves, skirts and dresses. Be sure to check the local weather in Provence and the Riviera for the time of year you're traveling and pack sweaters, jackets, or coats accordingly. It's always a good idea to **pack an umbrella or raincoat and clothes for layering** in cooler weather, and a good pair of **walking shoes** that you'll be comfortable in (preferably water-resistant if you're traveling in colder months; comfortable, light sandals or sneakers to walk good distances in the warmer weather).

• If you're planning on visiting any of the beautiful cathedrals of France, bring **clothes that appropriately cover** your shoulders and legs.

• **A backpack** can be handy during the day when you go out sightseeing and collecting souvenirs, particularly when getting on and off buses, boats, trains or trams.

• **If you don't speak French**, be sure to pack a good **conversational French phrase guide** to bring along with you. You'll find people a lot friendlier toward you if you don't go around assuming they speak your language.

• **Hand sanitizer** is always great to have along with you when traveling.

• A simple **first aid kit** is always a good idea to have in your luggage, just in case.

• **Medication.** Don't forget to have enough for the duration of your trip. It's also helpful to have a **note from your physician** if you're concerned about being questioned about carrying a certain quantity. And don't forget your **allergy pills** if you're prone. Make sure to bring enough of it with you and bring **a note from your doctor** if you are suffering from a condition that others need to be aware of.

• Bring one or two **reusable shopping bags** for trips to the grocery store and for carrying souvenirs home.

• Be sure to **leave expensive jewels and high-priced electronics at home**. Like most major cities and tourist attractions, thieves and pickpockets abound in tourist areas. Avoid making yourself a target.

✓ Phone Home

How will you call home from France? Does your cell phone company offer service while abroad? **What are their rates?**

There are many ways to **call home** from France that are inexpensive or completely free.

You may also **sign up for roaming or Internet hotspot** through your own cell phone provider. You can also use Skype, WhatsApp, Viper, or many other voice-over IP providers that are entirely free.

Other options are to buy a **French phone chip** for your phone—which also gives you a French phone number—purchase calling codes before you leave home, or you can buy calling cards or **prepaid cell phones** once you arrive in France.

✓ Currency Exchange

The currency in France is the euro so you'll need to exchange your $ for €. It's a good idea to have **at most 200 euros** to pay for transportation, tipping, and any other travel expense you may incur.

France is considered one of the more expensive countries to visit, so it's good to be prepared. ATMs are readily available and you'll get the exchange rate on the day of withdrawal. You can **check current exchange** rates online using the following or many other online currency exchange calculators, or through your bank: http://www.xe.com/currencyconverter

In France, **currency exchange** is offered in banks, post offices, airports, and even in some hotels. You can also find exchanges in some department stores and railway stations. **Please note** that exchange rates are fixed, but commission rates are flexible. Hotels and airports usually have much higher commissions.

Unless it can't be avoided, **never carry more than €200** in cash on you at a time; this will minimize your losses in the event of theft.

Make sure your bank knows you'll be traveling abroad. This way you avoid having foreign country transactions flagged and declined, which can be extremely inconvenient.

✓ Contact Your Embassy

In the unfortunate event you should lose your passport or be victimized while in France, **your country's embassy** will be able to help you. Be sure to give your itinerary and contact information to a **close friend or family member**, then also contact your embassy with your emergency contact information before you leave home.

✓ Your Mail

Ask a neighbor to **check your mailbox** while you're away or visit your local post office and request a hold. **Overflowing mailboxes** are a dead giveaway that no one's home.

• Getting in the Mood •

Here are a few great books and films set in Provence or the French Riviera that we recommend you watch in preparation for your trip to these **magical locales!**

What to Read:

A Year in Provence and *Toujours Provence*. Peter Mayle's works have been translated into a number of languages and are a staple for reading up on Provence, France.

What to Watch:

Alfred Hitchcock's well-known romantic comedy *To Catch a Thief*, features both the French Riviera and phenomenal performances by Grace Kelly and Cary Grant. Cary Grant plays a retired jewel burglar preying on the wealthy visitors of the Riviera. We think it's definitely worth watching prior to your trip to France!

Another interesting movie to watch is ***Swimming Pool***, a French-British thriller set in Provence. It's about a British crime novelist who travels to her publisher's summer home in the South of France, seeking solitude to work on a book. But an unexpected visitor arrives and complicates things. It's a good one!

We hope you'll enjoy getting in the mood for France!

• Local Tourist Information •

Regional tourism authorities have a strong presence on the ground here and can provide lots of useful information. So **once you arrive**, you can seek out their offices for maps, directions, and a healthy dose of supplemental recommendations, which always compliments your travel guides!

Be sure to **call ahead or visit their websites** for the most current hours of operation.

The main **tourist offices** we recommend are:

Provence Tourist Office
http://www.aixenprovencetourism.com
Address: 300 Avenue Giuseppe Verdi, 13100 Aix-en-Provence, France
Phone Number: +33 (0) 4 42 161 161

Marseille Tourist Office
http://www.marseille-tourisme.com
Address: 11 la Canebiere - 13001 Marseille
Phone Number: +33 (0) 826 500 500

Cannes Tourist Office
http://www.cannes-destination.com
Address: 1 Boulevard de la Croisette, 06400, Cannes
Phone Number: +33 (0) 4 92 99 84 22

Nice Tourist Office
http://www.nicetourisme.com
Address: 5 Promenade des Anglais, BP 4079, 06302, Cedex 4, Nice
Phone Number: +33 (0) 892 707 407

St. Tropez Tourist Office
http://fr.sainttropeztourisme.com
Address: 8 Quai Jean Jaues, 83990 Saint-Tropez
Phone Number: +33 (0) 892 68 48 28

Monaco Tourist Office
http://www.visitmonaco.com
Address: 2a Boulevard des Moulins, 98000, Monaco
Phone Number: +377 (0) 92 16 61 16

• About the Airports •

Depending on the region of Provence and the French Riviera you choose to visit, there are several choices to fly into:

• **Western Provence** (Avignon, Aix, Arles, Luberon, Ventoux, Camargue) is served by three airports: **Avignon Caumont Airport** (a small and friendly airport typically sees European travelers):
http://www.avignon.aeroport.fr/en, **Nimes Air-port:** http://www.aeroport-nimes.fr/home, and **Marseille-Provence Airport:** http://www.marseille-airport.com

• **Central Provence** (Var département, coast from the Rhône to St. Tropez) has two convenient airports: **Marseille-Provence Airport** as previously mentioned, and **Toulon-Hyères Airport:**
http://www.toulon-hyeres.aeroport.fr/en

• **Eastern and Northern-most area of Provence** (Digne, Alpes-de-Haute-Provence, Verdon Gorges) are accessible from **Nice-Côte-d'Azur International Airport:**
http://en.nice.aeroport.fr

• How Long is the Flight? •

The Flight to Nice:

• from **London** is approx. **2 hours**

• from **Moscow** is approx. **4 hours**

• from **NYC** is approx. **8.5 hours**

• from **Sydney** is approx. **24 hours**

• from **Hong Kong** is approx. **15 hours**

• from **Cape Town** is approx. **15.5 hours**

The Flight to Marseille:

• from **London** is approx. **2 hours**

• from **Moscow** is approx. **5.5 hours**

• from **NYC** is approx. **10.5 hours**

- from **Sydney** is approx. **26 hours**

- from **Hong Kong** is approx. **15.5 hours**

- from **Cape Town** is approx. **15 hours**

• Overview of Provence & the French Riviera •

A trip to Provence (once a province of ancient Rome) **and the French Riviera** can be a truly unforgettable experience!

You'll dine fabulously and be immersed in the powerful impressionist culture, festivals, and **romantic allure**.

In its prime, **the world-famous French Riviera** (Côte d'Azur) attracted movie stars, Russian billionaires and the like, but now the jet set atmosphere offers a more laid back feel, with an **easygoing cafe culture** you're sure to love!

With short hikes most days (less than three hours), you can see this beautiful land from a very **distinct perspective**. Sample some of the incredible **French wines** exactly where they're made. Inhale fragrant **lavender scents** everywhere you go. Dine in the great outdoors and in the finest restaurants. Stay in **cozy and luxu-**

rious 5-star hotels. Try your luck over in **Monte Carlo.**

Visit ancient Roman ruins, **medieval fortresses** and beautiful **hilltop Provençal villages**. Hike the Grand Canyon du Verdon or ride the **famous white horses** in the Camargue. See Avignon, Saint Rémy, Arles, the Luberon and Alpilles mountains.

Smile. The **magic and allure** awaits!

• Insider Tips For Tourists •

Etiquette

The French really don't deserve their infamous reputation for being rude. Many in particular are sticklers for sophistication and formality, so American-style manners are considered informal and impolite.

The first thing you should ask when engaging someone is: "Do you speak English?" That's sure to get you off on better footing than initially approaching someone *in English*...and even better if you actually **say it in French:** "Parlez-vous Anglais?" (parlay-voo onglay?)

Before you go, or during your flight, etc, take the time to learn a few common French words and phrases you'll need for interacting with shop attendants, street vendors, etc.

Always greet with **bonjour** (bohn-jhoor), which means "Hello" or "Good day," when you go into a hotel, store, shop or café; and *au revoir* (orhuv-whar) "Goodbye" whenever you leave, no matter who seems to be paying attention to you. Sometimes only a few people will respond, while at other times everyone will!

When addressing a female who's over the age of 16 use *madame* (ma-dam), which means, "My lady." For younger girls, use *mademoiselle* (mad-mwa-zel), which means "miss."

It's *monsieur* (muh-syur) for both boys and men alike.

Be sure you always say please, *s'il vous plaît* (see-voo-play), and thank you, *merci* (mehr-see).

Dining Etiquette: The French are very passionate about food and dining etiquette (particularly in fine restaurants) is very important in France.

This isn't Italy—be sure you **arrive on time** for dinner reservations.

Avoid asking for hard liquor or cocktails (especially martini or scotch) before dinner, as it's viewed as palate numbing and spoils the dining experience.

Never cut bread with a knife—always break it with your hands.

Table manners are Continental: while eating, the fork is held in the left hand and the knife in the right. When you're finished eating, place your knife and fork side by side on the plate at the 5:25 position.

Eating while walking down the street is generally frowned upon.

Social Interaction Etiquette: The French are quite reserved people and **highly value their privacy**. So do not ask personal questions related to occupation, salary, age, family or children unless you have a well-established friendship, or they begin volunteering that information first.

Also, **first names** are reserved for family and close friends. Wait until invited before using someone's first name.

Greeting Etiquette: If you know someone well, you may greet him or her with two kisses, one on each cheek. Otherwise, a handshake is best. The French **don't do hugs** and might be uncomfortable if you hug them.

Bathroom Etiquette: Avoid excusing yourself to use the restroom in the middle of a meal.

Time Zone

All of France is in the Central European Time Zone (UTC + 1:00). There is a six-hour time difference between New York City and France (France is ahead). When it's 8:00 am in New York City, it is 2:00 pm in France.

The format for abbreviating dates in Europe is different from the US. They use: **day/month/year**. So for example, August 23, 2019 is written in Europe as 23 August 2019, or 23/8/19.

Saving Time & Money

Since Provence and the French Riviera is one of the world's most visited (and crowded) regions, you're likely to have a better experience if you **make certain preparations** well in advance. Whenever possible, buy tickets for just about everything online: most of the museums and cultural centers sell tickets in advance. There may be a minimal service fee but it's well worth it to avoid spending all your time waiting in lines.

When looking for a place to stay, check out **Gites de France.** They feature listings for a variety of **low-cost accommodations** throughout France. *Chambres d'hotes* are the French version of the bed and breakfast; self-catering *gites* allow visitors to rent apartments, villas, or houses: http://en.gites-de-france.com

Plan a picnic for lunch a few days—or even dinner—instead of dining in restaurants. French cheeses, bread, pastries, and wines are delicious no matter where you buy and consume them. It will be less expensive if you buy them in a shop rather than in a café or restaurant.

Shop for your transportation online. The French transportation system is such that you can pay different prices for seats in the same train compartment. It all depends on when and where you purchase them. **Shop around**, try different departure days and times if possible—just as with airlines—and see if you can reduce the price of your travel. And remember: we always recommend **buying train tickets** in advance.

Tipping

By law, bills in restaurants and bars must include service (some servers may tell you otherwise but don't believe them), so you **do not** have to tip, however it is polite to round your bill up a couple euros if you're happy with the service. **Use your discretion**—for a beer you may leave an extra €0.25, for a meal you might leave €1–€3.

In high-end restaurants (such as those we recommend later in this guide) it's customary to leave a 5% tip on the table.

Tip **taxi drivers and hairstylists** 10% of the bill.

After **lengthy road trips,** you should tip the bus driver about €2.

After **guided tours,** tip the guide about 10% of the price of the tour.

Watch out for signs that say *pourboire interdit* — tipping banned/forbidden; otherwise you can tip theater and hotel cloakroom attendants €0.50, but they usually expect nothing.

If you're in a hotel for more than two or three days, leave about €1–€2 per day for the maid. It's appropriate to tip €2 (€1 in a moderately priced hotel) to whoever carries your bags or hails your taxi. **For room service**, give €1–€2 to the server (with the exception of routine breakfast).

If the maid does **pressing or laundering** for you, tip her €1.50–€2.

If the **concierge** was helpful, leave a tip of €5–€15, at your own discretion.

When You Have to Go

To ask **where the restroom** is in French: "Où sont les toilettes?" (Remember it's considered rude to excuse yourself to use the restroom during a meal.)

Department stores, **fast-food chains and public parks** are all good places to find **clean** public toilets.

Train, metro stations, upscale clubs and restaurants often have restroom attendants who keep them clean, so it's a good idea to have change on you when using these facilities.

If you happen to be **out sightseeing** and need to use the restroom, the easiest thing to do is dash into a coffee shop. Just **ask politely**: "Est-ce que je peux utiliser vos toilettes, s'il vous plaît?" (May I use your restroom?) with a smile and you're good to go.

Although they've become scarce, it's possible to run into **Turkish-style toilets** — a mere hole in the ground. **When you flush these**, step as far away as you can to avoid having the water splash your shoes or clothes.

Sometimes the light in a bathroom comes on only once the cubicle door is closed and locked. They often work on a timer to save on electricity, 3 minutes tops. **So if the light goes off** before you're finished, simply press the button again.

Taxes

By law, affixed prices in France must include taxes. Restaurants and hotels must include all service charges and taxes in their prices. If you ever see these as additional charges on a bill, do not pay it before addressing it with a manager.

There is one exception, with hotels and other lodging accommodations: you may see a tourist tax or *taxe de séjour* added to your bill at checkout time that can range anywhere from €0.20 to €1.50 per person, per day.

V.A.T.—Value-Added Tax is known in France as *taxe sur la valeur ajoutée,* or TVA. As of this writing, the standard rate is 20%. **Luxury goods** are taxed up to 33%; food in restaurants 10%. TVA tax for services is not refundable, but foreigners can get a TVA refund on products and goods. The item/s must be purchased for €175.01 on a single day in a participating shop (watch for the 'Tax-Free' notice on the door or window).

Obtain VAT refunds through the PABLO system. Here's how it works: Retailers that participate will give you a computer-generated PABLO V.A.T. refund form with a barcode. When you get to the airport, **before you check-in your luggage,** you need to scan your barcode at a PABLO machine to get the refund credited to your bank account. Service is provided in English.

The most common European V.A.T. refund system is **Global Blue.** Watch for their sign when shopping. Their service provides refunds in a variety of options:  credit card adjustment, check or cash.

Phone Calls

The country code for France is 33. When calling into France from outside the country, you drop the first 0 from the number. For example, the number for the Notre-Dame Cathedral is 1-42-34-56-10. To call this number from Miami, you would dial 00-33-1-42-34-56-10. **But to call from within France**, you dial 01-42-34-56-10.

When calling home from Provence, first dial 00 after which you'll hear a tone. Then dial the country code (1 for the US and Canada, 44 for the UK, 61 for Australia and 64 for New Zealand, 52 for Mexico, 7 for Russia, 86 for China, 81 for Japan), then the area code without the initial 0, then the number.

It's often expensive to call internationally, especially if you do so from a hotel phone. They almost always add surcharges.

Buying **local calling cards** can keep staying in touch less of an expense.

Prepaid cell phones can be bought in France at a rate of about €0.70/minute to call the US or Canada. Depending on the provider, the rest of the world can be nearly double. Incoming calls are usually free.

If you decide to **bring your own cell phone**, check with your provider on coverage and rates. Texting internationally tends to be less expensive. You can also use Skype, WhatsApp, Viper, or many other voice over IP providers that are entirely free.

Most **landlines in France** include service plans that cover international calls, but it's a good idea to **verify this** before making calls if you're renting an apartment.

If you want to **reach an operator** for help placing a call, **dial 08-00-99-00** (toll free) together with the last two digits of the country's code. So for help calling the US and Canada from Paris, you would dial 08-00-99-00-11. For England you would dial: 08-00-99-00-44. For Mexico you would dial 08-00-99-00-52.

Electricity

Electricity in France, as in the rest of Europe, is at **220 volts** alternating at 50 cycles per second (to compare, in the U.S. it's 110 volts, alternating at 60 cycles per second.)

As discussed before, when traveling from outside of Europe you will need to bring an adapter and converter that enable you to plug your electronics and appliances into the sockets they use. Cell phone, tablet and laptop chargers are **typically dual voltage**, so you won't need a converter, just an adapter to be able to plug it in.

Most small appliances are likely to be dual voltage, but **always double check** when possible, especially to avoid frying things like hair dryers and travel irons that weren't built for the higher voltage used in Europe.

In Emergencies

In an emergency, call 112 from your mobile device. 112 is an emergency phone number for all emergencies within the countries of the European Union. 17 is an emergency number for police in France. 18 is for fire department, and 15 is for medical help (SAMU).

French Phrases For Emergencies:

Au feu!	Fire!
Cherchez un médecin/un doc- teur!	Get a doctor!
Je suis malade.	I'm sick.
Police!	Police!
Au secours!	Help!
Appelez une ambulance!	Call an ambu- lance!

Holidays

There are a number of public holidays in France, but the most important, national holiday is **Bastille Day**. In France, it is formally called La Fête Nationale (The National Celebration) and celebrated on July 14. The

French National Day commemorates the start of the French Revolution with the Storming of the Bastille on July 14, 1789.

Date	Holiday name	Holiday type
Jan 1	New Year's Day	National holiday
March or April	Easter	Local holiday
May 1	Labor Day / May Day	National holiday
May 8	WWII Victory Day	National holiday
May 14	Ascension Day	National holiday
May 24	Whit Sunday	Observance
May 25	Whit Monday	National holiday
May 31	Mother's Day	Observance

Date	Holiday name	Holiday type
Jul 14	Bastille Day	National holiday
Aug 15	Assumption of Mary	National holiday
Nov 1	All Saints' Day	National holiday
Nov 11	Armistice Day	National holiday
Dec 24	Christmas Eve	Observance
Dec 25	Christmas Day	National holiday
Dec 26	St Stephen's Day	Local holiday
Dec 31	New Year's Eve	Observance

Hours of Operation

Banks in France are open between 9:00 am and 6:30 or 5:00 pm, Monday through Friday. Provençal banks are usually open at 8:00 am and close at 6:30 pm, Tuesday through Saturday. Some banks close during lunch (between 1:00 and 3:00 pm).

Most **stores** are open from 10:00 am until 7:00 pm (grocery stores open earlier). In larger cities, some stores **remain open until 10:00 pm.** In the south of France, they will often **close for lunch** between 1:00 and 3:00 pm.

Most of **museums** in France are closed on Mondays, but stay open longer during the summer months.

Government offices and businesses are usually 9:00 am - 5:00 pm.

Money

France uses the euro (€) as its currency (same as most of Western and Central Europe). Check out the currency exchange rates prior to your trip. You can do so online using the following or many other online currency exchange calculators, or through your bank: http://www.xe.com/currencyconverter

Debit and credit cards are accepted in most stores, hotels, restaurants, and service stations in France. Brands like American Express, Visa, and MasterCard are most commonly accepted. There is often a **minimum purchase** requirement of €15.

Tourist areas will have higher pricing than any others. So don't expect to save money in boutiques, restaurants or hotels around, say, the Rothschild villa or the Carrières de Lumières areas.

Climate and Best Times to Travel

Of course, Provence and the French Riviera enjoy **very sunny weather** most of the year; the climate is considered Mediterranean.

Spring and autumn are the best times to travel when temperatures are most comfortable and there are fewer crowds of tourists.

Summer is festival time, and the weather tends to be dry and hot. Many Europeans vacation in **July and August**, jamming up the Riviera.

In September they have the grape harvest, and small wineries are closed to wine-tasting tourists. Late autumn sees scenic greenery and a tranquil atmosphere.

Although the weather can be almost perfect despite the season, Provence has been known to dip down to **chilling wind chills in the winter**. The winds play a key role in the region's climate.

Visiting during winter is fine, but keep in mind that tourist information offices tend to be open for fewer hours at this time of year, and many tourist activities **go on hiatus**.

Transportation

Public transportation is excellent in France. The **TER** (Transport Express Régional) train runs along the coast and provides regular service to all coastal towns between Saint-Raphaël and Ventimiglia.

If you want to **cover as much ground** as possible during your stay, you can travel around very inexpensively by bus. There's a **nighttime bus service** that runs 3 nights a week, and on the evening before all national holidays. It departs out of Nice, and takes passengers to Monaco, Menton, and Cannes.

Driving

The highway system in France is quite good, not hard to navigate (the only place in France where driving can be challenging is Paris).

Roads are marked in the following categories: Autoroute (Motorway), which has red number signs. Signs with a letter "N" mean the National roads; "D" means the Departmental roads (yellow number signs). You might also encounter "municipal" (white number sign) and "forest" roads (green signs).

Print out your driving directions ahead of time, or ensure your rental car has an English-language GPS, and it shouldn't be difficult for you to navigate the French roadways.

• Tours •

We've got a few awesome recommendations for experiencing Provence and the Riviera. Be sure to **check the websites** or call for current rates and advanced booking.

By Bike

We recommend **Discover France Adventures' <u>Gordes Provencal Escape</u> bike tour** through Provence. You'll spend four nights in Gordes, at a hotel of your choice with different itinerary options for exploring the surrounding villages and beautiful panoramas of Provence. The level of difficulty is tailored to accommodate your speed preference and physical fitness.

Discover France Adventures
Phone Number: +800 929 0152 or +33 (0) 4 67 15 82 00
Visit: <u>http://www.discoverfrance.com/tours/self-guided/cycle/gordes-provencal-escape</u>

Another great option is **Discover France Adventures' Provence Secrets**. This is a **self-guided cycle tour** that offers insight to history and charm: Nimes, St. Remy, Vincent Van Gogh and his life in Provence, the Provençal markets, etc. It's a phenomenal five-day experience — definitely worth trying!

Discover France Adventures
Phone Number: +800 929 0152 or +33 (0) 4 67 15 82 00
Visit: http://www.discoverfrance.com/tours/self-guided/cycle/provence-secrets

By Boat

We think one of the best ways to **experience the French Riviera** is on a 4-hour **boat tour!** We recommend **Excursions Acti Loisirs**. It starts at Villefranche-sur-Mer (near Nice) and makes its way towards the Côte d'Azur, sighting dolphins and whales in the Mediterranean. This tour typically runs from June to September.

Phone Number: +33 601 33 42 68
http://en.nicetourisme.com/practical-advice/398 and http://www.dauphin-mediterranee.com

Another one we love is the **Provence Sightseeing Tour: Marseille and Cassis Calanques Cruise.** This 6-hour tour offers the best views of Marseille and Cassis, with an expert guide. Embarking from Marseille, this tour takes you along the Corniche des Crêtes road, then stops in Cape Canailles for **views of the French Riviera**!

Phone Number: +888 651 9785
http://www.viator.com/tours/Marseille/Provence-Sightseeing-Tour-Marseille-and-Cassis-Calanques-Cruise/d485-3547MARSEILLECASSIS

It's impressive to view **Avignon's great landmarks** from the River Rhone. **Grands Bateaux de Provence** offers several river excursions, including trips between Avignon and Villeneuve-lès-Avignon, along with fabulous dinner cruises.

Phone Number: +33 (0) 4 90 85 62 25
http://www.avignon-et-provence.com/mireio

By Bus

Provence Vision (Lieutaud) offers the best full day or half-day **bus tours** into the Provençal countryside, departing daily in the summer from Avignon Central Station. Tours include great stops for **shopping and sightseeing**.

Phone Number: +33 (0) 4 90 86 36 75
http://www.cars-lieutaud.fr

Try Special Interest or Walking Tours

We just love the **Provence Epicurean Adventure** wine tours! It's such great stimulation for the senses. The tour begins with a 3-night stay in Avignon, then 2 nights in Aix en Provence. Includes breakfast, wine tastings, a private guide through the vineyards, transportation, and even cooking classes. Enjoy!

Phone Number: +866 313 2856
http://www.enchanted-france.com/EF-DetailPages/GOOGLE_PROVENCE-EPICUREAN.html

Best of France Travels offers a comprehensive **9-day package tour** of Provence and the French Riviera that we think is several shades of awesome! They'll meet you at the airport in Nice, and then following a fabulously jam-packed 9-day itinerary, return you in time for your bittersweet departure.

Phone Number: +33 06 7746 4644
http://bestoffrancetravels.com/provence-the-riviera

• 5 Days in Provence & the French Riviera! •

Enjoy this 5-day itinerary for a well-balanced and easy-going, Provençal experience! Modify or adjust if you like, we have several options given in the **upcoming sections** on budget and luxury hotel recommendations, and for enjoying nightlife and theater in each city—and always keep in mind that it's best to buy your tickets and make reservations ahead of time whenever possible. **Check websites** and/or **call** for the current rates and hours of operation.

• Day 1 •

Why not begin your trip in beautiful **Marseille** (pronounced: mar-say)? It's France's oldest city and the capital of Provence. With numerous train, bus and plane connections, it's also one of France's greatest transportation hubs.

Fly into Marseille Provence Airport and check into your hotel for a quick rest; get **refreshed and renewed** before heading back out to explore! Marseille may not look like the charming Provençal villages you're about to enjoy, but its rich history makes it quite a treat. And it's not a long way from anything...

If you go forty-five minutes east, you're in the French Riviera; a half-hour north takes you to the heart of Provence and the amazing towns of Avignon, Arles, Aix and Orange.

If you arrive in the morning, spend it strolling down to see the famed **Old Port of Marseille** (*Vieux Port* in French). Cross the port to **Le Panier**, one of the oldest and most authentic districts in the city, then many visitors like to take the metro up to **Cours Julien**, one of the more vibrant areas of Marseille!

In the afternoon, grab lunch (see our **top recommendations ahead**), and then hop a boat to the **Château d'If**, the infamous island upon which Alexandre Dumas set his legendary novel: "The Count of Monte Cristo."

If you have time and aren't too tired, visit **The Abbey of St. Victor** (Basilique Saint-Victor).

However, if religious buildings aren't your thing, another great place to visit in Marseille is **Palais du Pharo**, an impressive waterfront the city gifted Napoleon III. Now a conference center, there are several meeting halls inside, and a splendid auditorium with the capacity for 900 people. You can take a guided tour or just peruse on your own.

For dinner tonight? We recommend the amazing **Le Chalet du Pharo**. Such delicious Mediterranean cuisine + breathtaking views of the Old Port! This is a very popular restaurant so it's best to make your reservations well in advance. You can also book online via their website.

Spend the night in Marseille, enjoying the city's bustling nightlife before turning in for a good night's sleep. We have **great recommendations ahead** if you're up for dancing and theater!

Location Information:

Old Port of Marseille
Address: At the end of the Canebière, the historic street in the old quarter of Marseille

Chateau d'If
Address: Embarcadère Frioul If, 1 Quai de la Fraternité, 13001, Marseille
Phone Number: +33 (0) 6 03 06 25 26
http://www.monuments-nationaux.fr

The Abbey of St. Victor
Address: Place Saint-Victor, 13007, Marseille
Phone Number: +33 (0) 4 96 11 22 60
http://www.saintvictor.net

Palais du Pharo
Address: 58 Boulevard Charles Livon, 13007, Marseille
Phone Number: +33 (0) 4 91 14 64 95
http://palaisdupharo.marseille.fr

Le Chalet du Pharo
Address: 58 Boulevard Charles Livon, Jardin du Pharo, 13007, Marseille
Phone Number: +33 (0) 4 91 52 80 11
http://www.le-chalet-du-pharo.com

• Day 2 •

On your second day, after breakfast at the hotel, we recommend grabbing your map and either taking a train or renting yourself a car and driving to **Avignon**. It's about an hour by car, and once you're there you won't want to leave, trust us. Avignon is one of *the* most charming French towns, rich with fascinating history, art, music, and special events for everyone.

Take a nice stroll through the town and explore the beautifully historic, narrow cobblestone streets. **The Old Avignon** area is rich in texture and worth far more of your time than the new town in our opinion.

In the morning, make your way over to the **Calvet Museum**, one of southern France's most engaging museums for archaeology and artistry. Featured artwork includes pieces by Manet, Monet, Sisley, Modigliani as well as lesser-known local artists who are definitely worth a look-see!

For lunch, we recommend **Restaurant l'Epicerie** the most; it's in the heart of Avignon in St. Peter's Square (and close to the spot we're sending you next, Palais des Papes).

After lunch, you must go over and see the large, open square in front of the **Palais des Papes,** and of course the palace itself. The square has 'round the clock **street entertainers**, year-round. Built Goth-style, **this Palace** was built for the pope during the 14th century Avignon Papacy. In addition to featuring a **distinguished art collection**, books, and artifacts, the Palace plays host to many world-renowned art exhibits.

Another must see site is **Musee Angladon**. This **art museum** was the former home of the heir to the Parisian couturier, and collector Jacques Doucet and **features several Picassos**, as well as other great paintings by Van Gogh, Manet, Sisley and several others.

For dinner in Avignon, we love **Le 46**, a very nice French restaurant that has delicious local dishes, is reasonably priced and has a cozy feel. We recommend reserving your table in advance.

Additionally, while the Colosseum in Rome is one of the most well known tourist attractions in the world, most people have never even heard of the **Arena of Nîmes**, a Roman amphitheatre built in 70 A.D. that is better preserved than the Colosseum and still in use today. **The amazing town of Nîmes** (pronounced: neem) is a mere 45-minute drive from Avignon. **Catch a concert during your visit, or a bullfight** and experience **spectatorship** from the viewpoint of your ancient counterparts!

The view from the top of the arena is **jaw-dropping** and makes a visit to **Nîmes, France** well worth your while.

Location Information:

Calvet Museum
Address: 65 Rue Joseph Vernet, 84000, Avignon, France
Phone Number: +33 (0) 4 90 86 33 84
http://www.musee-calvet-avignon.com

Restaurant l'Epicerie
Address: 10 Place Saint-Pierre, 84000, Avignon
Phone Number: +33 (0) 4 90 82 74 22
http://www.restaurantlepicerie.fr

Palais des Papes
Address: Place du Palais, 84000, Avignon
Phone Number: +33 (0) 4 32 74 32 74
http://www.palais-des-papes.com

Musee Angladon
Address: 5 rue Laboureur, Avignon
Phone Number: + 33 (0) 4 90 82 29 03
http://www.angladon.com

Le 46 Restaurant
Address: 46 rue de la Balance, 84000, Avignon
Phone Number: +33 (0) 4 90 85 24 83

Arena of Nîmes
Address: Boulevard des Arènes, 30000 Nîmes, France
Phone Number: +33 4 66 21 82 56
http://arenes-nimes.com

An Alternative Itinerary (Day 2):

On your second day, after a nice breakfast at your hotel, you could also take the train to the town of **Orange**. (Or, you could spend half a day in Avignon and the second half in Orange.) Orange (Occitan) is about 13 miles north of Avignon. We like taking the train, but you can also take the bus or a cab.

Orange is celebrated for its **great theatre and Roman architecture**. **The Roman Theater Orange** (Théâtre antique d'Orange), is one of the best-preserved antiquities of the Holy Roman Empire. And the dazzling **Triumphal Arch of Orange** is inscribed with a dedication to the emperor Tiberius in AD 27—definitely go see it!

For lunch in Orange, head over to **La Dinette**. It's really good, fresh food in a cozy setting.

France is quite known for its great wineries, so while in Orange, don't miss a visit to one of the nearby wineries. Enjoy a taste of some of the **greatest French wines**. We recommend **Vignobles Alain Jaume & Fils**. It's such a charming winery and offers wine tastings and gorgeous views of the French countryside.

And if you fancy a later stay in Orange, don't miss our **theater recommendation** ahead.

Location Information:

Théâtre antique d'Orange
Address: Rue Madeleine Roch, 84100, Orange, France
Phone Number: +33 (0) 4 90 51 17 60
http://www.theatre-antique.com

Triumphal Arch of Orange
Address: Avenue de l'Arc de Triomphe, 84100, Orange
Phone Number: +33 (0) 4 90 34 70 88
http://www.otorange.fr

La Dinette
Address: 7 Bis, rue Victor Hugo, 84100, Orange
Phone Number: +33 (0) 4 90 66 90 38
https://www.facebook.com/Ladinetteorange

Vignobles Alain Jaume & Fils Winery
Address: 1358 route de Chateauneuf du Pape, 84100, Orange
Phone Number: +33 (0) 4 90 34 68 70
http://vignobles-alain-jaume.com

• Day 3 •

After a good night's rest, grab break-
fast at your hotel and then take a
bus, train, or car to the French Riviera's beautiful city of **Nice** (pronounced:
neece), just a 2.5-hour drive from
Marseille.

In addition to the **world-famous
beaches**, the city features awesome
museums, churches and ancient ru-
ins. Experiencing everything in one day won't be possible, so **you have a choice to make for today:** spend
the day relaxing on one of Nice's gorgeous sandy beaches, or you can choose to go sightseeing and discover
some of Nice's architectural gems, and museums featuring some of the most incredible artwork. **Either
choice** will be great! (However, if you can lengthen your
vacation, **spend two days** in Nice and do both!)

If you decide to sight-see, some of the must-see places in our opinion include: the breathtaking views from
Nice's Castle Hill (there's a free lift and elevator in
Nice Old Town), **Chagall Museum**, **Matisse Museum**, and **Museum of Modern and Contemporary Art**,
among others. There are also many great restaurants,
food stands (you must try some local **socca**!), bars,
and nightlife venues in Nice if you choose to stay
overnight.

For lunch in Nice, we like **Chez Acchiardo** in Nice
Old Town (*Le Vieux Nice* in France), a picturesque,
historic district of narrow streets, shops, markets and

restaurants. It's become very touristy in recent years so we've noticed tourist-geared pricing, but think **the authenticity of Old Town** still rests beneath this veneer.

If you stay for dinner, we say be spontaneous with your choice today. Try a restaurant in the area you're in and see how you like it, but **keep these tips in mind:** 1) as a rule of thumb, the better the veneer in Nice, the worse the food, when the food is good, they don't need fancy furniture to pull you in, and 2) the spots with older waiters and waitresses tend to be family run and have the better food.

Don't miss our other **dining options** and **nightlife recommendations** ahead. Enjoy your time in Nice!

Location Information:

Chagall Museum
Address: 36 Avenue Docteur Ménard, 06000, Nice
Phone Number: +33 (0) 4 93 53 87 20
http://en.musees-nationaux-alpesmaritimes.fr

Matisse Museum
Address: 164 Avenue des Arenes de Cimiez, 06000, Nice
Phone Number: +33 (0) 4 93 81 08 08
http://www.musee-matisse-nice.org

Museum of Modern and Contemporary Art
Address: Place Yves Klein, 06364, Nice
Phone Number: +33 (0) 4 97 13 42 01
http://www.mamac-nice.org

Chez Acchiardo
Address: 38 Rue Droite, 06300, Nice
Phone Number: +33 (0) 4 93 85 51 16
https://www.facebook.com/pages/Restaurant-Chez-Acchiardo/247157661974943

• Day 4 •

On your forth day, if still in Nice, you can take a quick, 20-minute train ride over to **Monaco** first thing in the morning (Monaco is a 3-hour drive from Marseille/half-hour drive from Nice). Monaco is an independent sovereign state on France's Mediterranean coastline. The **ritzy casinos**, swanky harbor full of big yachts owned by the wealthiest people on the planet, the Grand Prix motor races—are all uniquely Monaco. And let's not forget the legendary Princess Grace Kelly!

The first place we want to send you to in Monaco, aside from the marvelous beaches, is the **Museum of Oceanography!** Prince Albert I opened the museum in 1910 and world-renowned explorer and naval officer Jacques-Yves Cousteau was director here from 1957 to 1988.

March 2010 marked its **100-year anniversary** celebration. Aquariums, natural history collections, a panoramic terrace—the Museum offers visitors a very unique, oceanic learning experience. This spot is especially noteworthy if you're traveling with children or teens. They will love this place! There's also a **restaurant** here that's perched 278 feet above sea level—perfect for **lunch in Monaco**.

Another spot we know you'll want at the top of your list is **Place du Casino.** It's the epitome of high class in **Monte Carlo**, and a definitive showcase of European glamour: luxurious villas and yachts, exclusive restaurants, models, celebrities and fashion icons. There are also many great theaters and bars should you choose to enjoy Monaco's **fabulous nightlife** and opt to stay overnight.

As featured in the James Bond movies, *Never Say Never Again* and *Golden Eye*, the **Monte Carlo Casino** opened in 1863 in an effort to bring tourists and income to Monaco—and the rest is history.

Looking for great, **Kodak moment views of Monaco?** Go check out **Rampe Majeure**. Climb the historic staircase while taking in the dynamite scenery from the harbor on your way up. Although steep, it's not a long climb and definitely worth the breathtaking views of Monaco from the top. The ramp leads up to the **Palace Square** with a bronze statue in honor of François Grimaldi, the founder of Monaco's royal dynasty.

At the end of your busy day in Monaco, relax at the **Princess Grace Rose Garden**. Built in honor of Grace Kelly, it **pleases the senses** with its dazzling plants, trees, and flowers. A great space for taking a break; just unwind and relax.

A great spot for dinner in Monaco is **Le Petit Bar.** Mediterranean-themed fare with delicious flavors and portions. It's not the most expensive place in town, and the service is quite friendly—we think you'll enjoy it.

And if you love nightlife and theater, you're in the right place. Don't miss our **top recommendations for Monaco** ahead.

Location Information:

Monte Carlo Casino
Address: Casino Monte-Carlo, Place du Casino, 98000, Monaco
Phone Number: +377 98 06 28 00
http://www.casinomontecarlo.com

Museum of Oceanography
Address: Avenue Saint-Martin, 98000, Monaco
Phone Number: +377 93 15 36 00
http://www.oceano.mc

Princess Grace Rose Garden
Address: Fontvieille, Monaco
Phone Number: +377 92 16 61 16
http://www.visitmonaco.com/en/Places-to-visit/Gardens/Fontvieille-Park-and-the-Princess-Grace-Rose-Garden

Le Petit Bar (Restaurant)
Address: 35 rue Basse, 98000, Monaco
Phone Number: +377 97 70 04 97

• Day 5 •

Spend your fifth day in **Antibes** (pronounced: on-teeb) or **Cannes** (Pronounced: can), or do both—both Antibes and Cannes are about a 40-minute train ride from Monaco and about 30 minutes apart from each other. We would urge you to **spend more time** in the less-hyped town of Antibes.

Like other cities along the French Riviera, **Antibes** offers beautiful beaches with lots of big yachts, but this city also has a fascinating **medieval Old Town**, and prominent museums worth checking out!

The Picasso Museum is a former castle that features almost 250 of Picasso's works. Of course, the majority of the paintings are Picasso's, but there are also great pieces from contemporary artists.

Grab lunch in the Antibes **covered food market** in Cours Massena, in the center of the Old Town. Here you'll find a great variety of fresh fruit and vegetables, cheeses, olives, hams and sausages—great picnic foods!

Antibes is well known for **producing roses**, and a great way to spend the afternoon is strolling along the rose bush path to the sea at **The Exflora Park**, a very nice public Mediterranean garden in Antibes with enchanting ponds and fountains.

And while you're here, be sure not to miss the wonderful **beaches**. Some resorts have private sand for guests, but there are several free beaches if you're not staying at a seaside resort—both the **Plage du Ponteil** (a more modest, compact and narrow beach) and **Plage de la Salis** (a lengthy, white-sand beach where you can rent kayaks and paddleboards) are very popular, so we highly recommend a nice stroll along the beaches of Antibes!

If you make a jaunt over to **Cannes**, we recommend heading over to the **Forville Market**. Not on the low cost end of the spectrum (it is Cannes, after all) but it's a wonderful spot for fresh local produce. Perfect for making a picnic happen in Cannes!

In Cannes, we also recommend the **Guided Tour of the Palais des Festivals et des Congres**, one of the most photographed sites in the world! You'll (literally) walk in the footsteps of Hollywood glamour, so have your walking shoes at the ready—there are lots of steps! Enjoy!

And so after you sniff out some great dinner and wine in Antibes (or Cannes), if this marks the end of your Provencal vacation, take a train or bus back to Marseille in time to rest up and head back home again from the Marseille-Provence airport.

Location Information:

In Antibes:

The Picasso Museum (Musee Picasso)
Address: Place Marijol, 06600, Antibes, France
Phone Number: +33 (0) 4 92 90 54 20
http://www.antibes-juanlespins.com/les-musees/picasso

The Exflora Park (Parc Exflora)
Address: Avenue de Cannes, 06160, Antibes
Phone Number: +33 (0) 4 97 21 42 60
http://www.antibes-juanlespins.com/parcs-jardin-espaces-boises/le-parc-exflora

Antibes Food Market (Marché Provencal)
Address: 27 Cours Massena, 06600, Antibes

In Cannes:

Forville Market (Marché Forville)
Address: 12 Rue Louis Blanc, 06400, Cannes
Phone Number: +33 (0) 4 92 99 84 22 (tourist office for current hours of operation)

Guided Tour of the Palais des Festivals et des Congres
Address: 1 Boulevard de la Croisette, 06400, Cannes (tour begins at tourist office)
Phone Number: +33 (0) 4 92 99 84 22 (tourist office for current rates and availability)
http://www.cannes-destination.com/guided-visits/visit-palais-festival-cannes

• Best Places For Travelers on a Budget •

Bargain Sleeps

Don't forget, **Gites de France** features listings of a variety of low-cost accommodations throughout France, a perfect way to find something inexpensive. (Chambres d'hotes are French versions of bed and breakfasts). You can rent an apartment, house or villa with self-catering gites.

Website: http://en.gites-de-france.com

In Nice, we recommend **Hôtel Villa La Tour**, a former 18th century convent that's been converted into a cozy hotel in the city center, just a 10-minute walk from the beach. Bedrooms overlook the Nice Old Town and there's a small garden on the roof guests can enjoy.

Hotel Villa La Tour
Address: 4 rue de la Tour, 06300, Nice, French Riviera
Phone Number: +33 (0) 4 93 80 08 15
http://www.villa-la-tour.com

In Marseille, the **Mama Shelter Hotel** is a budget-friendly hotel that offers trendy urban designs from Philippe Stark, very futuristic-themed rooms, with a pastis specialty bar. The décor here is too cool to miss!

Mama Shelter Hotel
Address: 64, rue de la Loubière, 13006, Marseille
Phone Number: +33 (0) 4 84 35 20 00
http://www.mamashelter.com

In St. Tropez, the B Lodge Hotel is one of the lowest cost hotels you'll find. The rooms are small but the Wi-Fi is free, the staff is helpful and friendly, and best of all, it's a mere ten minutes from the heart of St. Tropez!

B Lodge Hotel
Address: 23 Rue de l'aioli, 83990, Saint-Tropez
Phone Number: +33 4 94 97 06 57
http://www.hotel-b-lodge.com

And while you can certainly do **Monaco** on a budget, it typically isn't easy to do it if you plan an overnight stay—it's much more economical to do the 20-minute train commute from Nice. However, for a nice accommodation that won't exactly blow your budget, we recommending staying at **Hotel de France**, a little hidden gem on the Riviera. It's small but clean and sufficient for a decent night's rest.

Hotel de France
Address: 6 rue de la Turbie, 98000, Monaco, French Riviera
Phone Number: +337 93 30 24 64

http://www.monaco-hotel.com/fr/hotels/monaco/hotel-de-france-monaco

The other option to getting the best of both worlds in **Monaco** is to step right over into **Beausoleil**, the middle-class town across the street where people who work in Monaco actually *live*. It's just a stone's throw from Monaco...seriously, it's right across the street! A stay at the **Azur Hotel** here in Beausoleil can set you back as little as €75 per night—a true bargain sleep on the French Riviera!

Azur Hotel Beausoleil
Address: 12 Boulevard de la République, 06240, Beausoleil, France
Phone Number: +33 (0) 4 93 78 01 25
http://www.azurhotelbeausoleil.com

Bargain Eats

Sur le Pouce is a simple and inexpensive but delicious Mediterranean restaurant near **Marseilles'** Vieux Port. Evenings are crowded, so it's best to book ahead and get there early.

Sur le Pouce
Address: 2 rue des Convalescents, 13001, Marseille
Phone Number: +33 (0) 4 91 56 13 28

In St. Tropez, our absolute favorite budget-friendly grub is at **Basilic Burger!** Their food is delicious, and a party of three can have a very nice meal here for well under €50, which is great for the area.

Basilic Burger
Address: Place des Remparts | 83990, Saint-Tropez
Phone Number: +33 4 94 97 29 09

Chez Pipo in **Nice** is where many locals go for their *socca.* You can enjoy tasty local specialties here, like pissaladière and tourte aux blettes. It's not the place to be if you're rushing. So just relax and enjoy the deliciousness!

Chez Pipo
Address: 13 rue Bavastro, Old Town, 06000, Nice
Phone Number: +33 (0) 4 93 55 88 82
http://www.chezpipo.fr

Delicious pizza can be found all over **Nice**, but we love and recommend the wood-fired Italian pizzas at **La Pizza Cresci.** It's delicious and it won't drain your budget. We recommend getting a table on the sidewalk—great people watching!

They are also located in **Cannes**, where menu prices are fair.

La Pizza Cresci (Nice)
Address: 34 rue Massena, 06000, Nice
Phone Number: + 33 (0) 4 93 87 70 29
http://maison-cresci.fr

La Pizza Cresci (Cannes)
Address: 3 Quai Saint-Pierre, 06400, Cannes
Phone Number: + 33 (0) 4 93 39 22 56
http://maison-cresci.fr

In Monaco, we recommend going into the nearby town of **Beausoleil** and checking out l'Alcazar for a nice, budget-friendly lunch.

l'Alcazar
Address: 3 boulevard General Leclerc, 06240, Beausoleil, France
Phone Number: +33 (0) 4 93 78 32 27
http://alcazar-restaurant.com

• Best Places For Ultimate Luxury •

Luxury Sleeps

<u>The Intercontinental Marseille-Hotel Dieu</u> is a luxury hotel in **Marseille** that offers a most elegant terrace, an award-worthy spa, and simply delectable dining in a grand 18th-century edifice. What's not to love?

The Intercontinental Marseille-Hotel Dieu
Address: 1 Daviel Square, 13002, Marseille
Phone Number: +33 (0) 4 13 42 42 42
<u>http://www.ihg.com/intercontinental/hotels/gb/e</u>
<u>n/marseille/mrsha/hoteldetail</u>

For ultimate luxury in St. Tropez, we recommend the wonderful **Hotel Sezz Saint-Tropez** a gorgeous boutique hotel with a great staff just waiting to pamper you when you walk through the door. The South of France has never felt this good!

Hotel Sezz Saint-Tropez
Address: 151 Route des Salins, 83990, Saint-Tropez
Phone Number: +33 4 94 55 31 55
http://saint-tropez.hotelsezz.com

For a luxurious stay in Nice, we love **Hotel la Perouse**. It's a fabulous location, right on the best beach in Nice; ultra clean when we were there, with views to die for. We recommend a junior suite!

Hotel la Perouse
Address: 11 Quai Rauba Capeu, 06300, Nice
Phone Number: +33 (0) 4 93 62 34 63
http://www.leshotelsduroy.com/en/hotel-la-perouse

And if you decide to stay overnight **in Monte Carlo**, obviously you're not short on superb luxury options, but one of the best in our opinion is **Hôtel Hermitage**. It's in the heart of **Monaco**, a stone's throw from the famed Monte Carlo casino and directly connected to the Thermes Marins Monte-Carlo, a world-famous luxury spa. With 5-star hospitality, a dining experience that's simply to die for, and some of the most breathtaking views in town, we know Hermitage will ensure you feel sufficiently spoiled, polished and pampered.

Hôtel Hermitage Monte-Carlo
Address: Square Beaumarchais, 98000, Monaco, French Riviera

Phone Number: +377 98 06 40 00
http://www.hotelhermitagemontecarlo.com

Luxury Eats

Marseille's <u>Le Petit Nice Passedat</u> is run by a father and son team, and it's one of the most popular restaurants in town. Enjoy fresh fish, delicate sea beignets, and a rather exotic soufflé! Be sure to make reservations for a table well in advance.

Le Petit Nice Passedat
Address: 17 rue des Braves, 13007, Marseille
Phone Number: +33 (0) 4 91 59 25 92
http://www.passedat.fr

In St. Tropez, we enjoy the quality cuisine and elegant atmosphere of **Restaurant Le G'**. It's a small and intimate atmosphere where taste is equally as important as presentation!

Restaurant Le G'
Address: 67 Rue du Portail Neuf, 83990, Saint-Tropez
Phone Number: +33 4 94 79 85 09
https://www.facebook.com/LeGRestaurant

In Nice, we know you'll love dining at **Les Sens.** A dining experience bursting with regional flavor, Les Sens is open daily for lunch and dinner and promises an unforgettably opulent feasting experience.

Les Sens
Address: 37 rue Pastorelli, 06100, Nice
Phone Number: +33 (0) 9 81 06 57 00
http://www.les-sens-nice.fr

Le Vauban in **Antibes** in Old Antibes is a delight among the numerous touristy restaurants and bars. Be sure to make reservations in advance and savor the wonderful experience of fine dining!

Le Vauban
Address: 7 Rue Thuret, 06600, Antibes
Phone Number: +33 4 93 34 33 05
http://levauban.fr

And even if you should choose to stay in another hotel in **Monaco**, we still recommend dining at the **Le Vistamar** restaurant in the Hôtel Hermitage. The dining experience here is exceptional, the food delicious, the selection of wine and liquor impressive. Be sure you make reservations well in advance.

Le Vistamar and Terrace
Address: Square Beaumarchais | Hôtel Hermitage, Monte-Carlo, 98000, Monaco
Phone Number: +377 98 06 98 98
http://www.montecarlosbm.com/restaurants-in-monaco/gourmet/vistamar

• Provence & the French Riviera Nightlife •

Great Bars in Provence & the French Riviera

A great spot for your jaunt to **Avignon** is the bar with a definite buzz: **Pub Z.** Owned by a rocker who's got a thing for zebras (as you'll notice), Pub Z stays open pretty late for this quiet town.

Pub Z
Address: 58 rue de la Bonneterie, 84000, Avignon
Phone Number: +33 (0) 4 90 85 42 84
https://www.facebook.com/pubz.avignon

In Monaco, you must visit the **Crystal Terrace Lounge** at the Hôtel Hermitage. Great spot for cocktails and drinks after dinner. Dress code is elegant, men must where jackets.

Crystal Terrace Lounge
Address: Square Beaumarchais | Hôtel Hermitage, Monte Carlo, 98000, Monaco
Phone Number: +377 98 06 98 99
http://www.montecarlosbm.com/bars-lounge-and-night-club/crystal-terrace

In Nice, a great "out of the way" locals champagne bar is **L'effervescence**. It serves good champagne, drinks and small plates of delicious light fare.

L'effervescence
Address: 10 rue de la Loge, 06300, Nice
Phone Number: +33 (0) 4 93 80 87 37
http://www.leffervescence-nice.com

Great Clubs in Provence & the French Riviera

If you're in the mood to dance while in **Marseille**, check out **Le New Orléans** dance club overlooking the old port. Competitions, dance classes, night themes of karaoke, salsa dance and disco—you'll have a ball.

Le New Orléans (Dance Club)
Address: 1, Quai Rîve Neuve, 13001, Marseille
Phone Number: +33 (0) 91 54 71 09

A great place **in Monaco** is **Flashman's Café**, a disco cocktail bar with a live DJ every night except Tuesdays when they're closed. It's an easy-going club atmosphere—the perfect place to dance, drink and stumble out of at dawn.

Flashman's Café
Address: 7 Avenue Princesse Alice, Monte Carlo, 98000, Monaco
Phone Number: +337 93 30 09 03

https://fr-fr.facebook.com/pages/Flashmans-
Café/161150920569445

Great Live Music in Provence & the French Riviera

Dock Des Suds is one of the best live music and night-club venues **in Marseille**. You can also find lots of fun cultural events here.

Dock Des Suds
Address: 12 Rue Urbain V, 13002, Marseille
Phone Number: +33 (0) 4 91 99 00 00
http://www.dock-des-suds.org

For great live music **in Nice**, visit **High Club/Studio 47**. Famous DJs and professional dancers hang out here. A more mature crowd parties at Studio 47, a smaller set adjacent to the High Club.

High Club/Studio 47
Address: 45 Prom. des Anglais, 06000, Nice
Phone Number: +33 (0) 6 16 95 75 87
http://www.highclub.fr

Great Theater in Provence & the French Riviera

We think **Theatre Toursky** in **Marseille** is a must-do if you love good theater. It's an intimate venue known for its moving performances.

Theatre Toursky
Address: 16 Prom. Léo Ferré, 13003 Marseille
Phone Number: +33 (0) 4 91 02 58 35
http://www.toursky.org

The town of **Orange in Provence** is equally well known for its great theater and the **Théâtre Antique d'Orange** is a very well preserved Roman theater. Theater buffs should certainly look into booking theater tickets here for their jaunt to visit Orange.

Théâtre Antique d'Orange
Address: Rue Madeleine Roch, 84100, Orange, France
Phone Number: +33 (0) 4 90 51 17 60
http://www.theatre-antique.com

The National Theatre of Nice has grown increasingly popular since it opened in 1989. You may catch some great performances during your visit to Nice.

The National Theatre of Nice
Address: Promenade des Arts, 06300, Nice
Phone Number: +33 (0) 4 93 13 90 90
http://www.tnn.fr

The **Monte Carlo Opera** is in a word: *spectacular*. Producing operatic performances since 1879, this opera house has staged many world-famous musical legends, including Placido Domingo, and Luciano Pavarotti.

Monte Carlo Opera
Address: Place du Casino, 98000, Monaco, French Riviera
Phone Number: + 377 98 06 28 00
http://www.opera.mc

We also recommend the **Theatre du Fort Antoine** in **Monte Carlo** for lots of outdoor productions from mid-July to mid-August in an open-air amphitheater that overlooks the Mediterranean. Theater participants also produce street shows all over Monte Carlo and Monaco.

Fort Antoine Theater
Address: Avenue de la Quarantaine, 98000, Monaco
Phone Number: + 377 98 98 83 03

• Conclusion •

We hope you've found our **guide to Provence and the French Riviera** helpful. A region filled with so many treasures, you'll undoubtedly have to come back again and again in order to thoroughly experience the best of it.

We wish you a **very safe and fun-filled trip** to Provence and the French Riviera!

Warm regards,

The Passport to European Travel Guides Team

Visit our Blog! Grab more of our signature guides for all your travel needs!

http://www.passporttoeuropeantravelguides.blogspot.com

★ **Join our mailing list** ★ to follow our Travel Guide Series. You'll be automatically entered for a chance to win a **$100 Visa Gift Card** in our monthly drawings! Be sure to respond to the confirmation e-mail to complete the subscription.

• About the Authors •

Passport to European Travel Guides is an eclectic team of international jet setters who know exactly what travelers and tourists want in a cut-to-the-chase, comprehensive travel guide that suits a wide range of budgets.

Our growing collection of distinguished European travel guides are guaranteed to give first-hand insight to each locale, complete with day-to-day, guided itineraries you won't want to miss!

We want our brand to be your official Passport to European Travel—one you can always count on!

Bon Voyage!

The Passport to European Travel Guides Team
http://www.passporttoeuropeantravelguides.blogspot.com

49313310R00046

Made in the USA
Columbia, SC
19 January 2019